I0392616

# Relax Range Book 4
# Dojo of Peace

Recharge Publishing

Copyright © 2016 Recharge Publishing

All rights reserved.

ISBN: **1537656031**
ISBN-13: **978-1537656038**

# DEDICATION

Firstly to my two besties, who I love so much and then to you for taking charge and giving yourself 5 minutes peace!
Enjoy!.

# CONTENTS

Message for you    i

Design 1        Pg #1

Design 2        Pg #3

Design 3        Pg #5

Design 4        Pg #7

Design 5        Pg #9

Design 6        Pg #11

Design 7        Pg #13

Design 8        Pg #15

Design 9        Pg #17

Design 10      Pg #19

Design 11      Pg #21

Design 12      Pg #23

Design 13      Pg #25

Design 14      Pg #27

Design 15      Pg #29

Design 16      Pg #31

Design 17      Pg #33

Design 18      Pg #35

Design 19      Pg #37

Design 20      Pg #39

Design 21      Pg #41

Design 22      Pg #43

Design 23      Pg #45

Design 24      Pg #47

Design 25      Pg #49

## MESSAGE FOR YOU

Life can be crazy sometimes and we often don't think about ourselves as much as we should each day. Whether it's a job, family, illness or something else, all things that take up your time and energy each day. To be the best in any situation you need to be focused and it's to easy to just go through the motions of the day each day. Take 5 minutes just for yourself! Recharge and go for it again. Your loved ones and your sole will thank you for it..

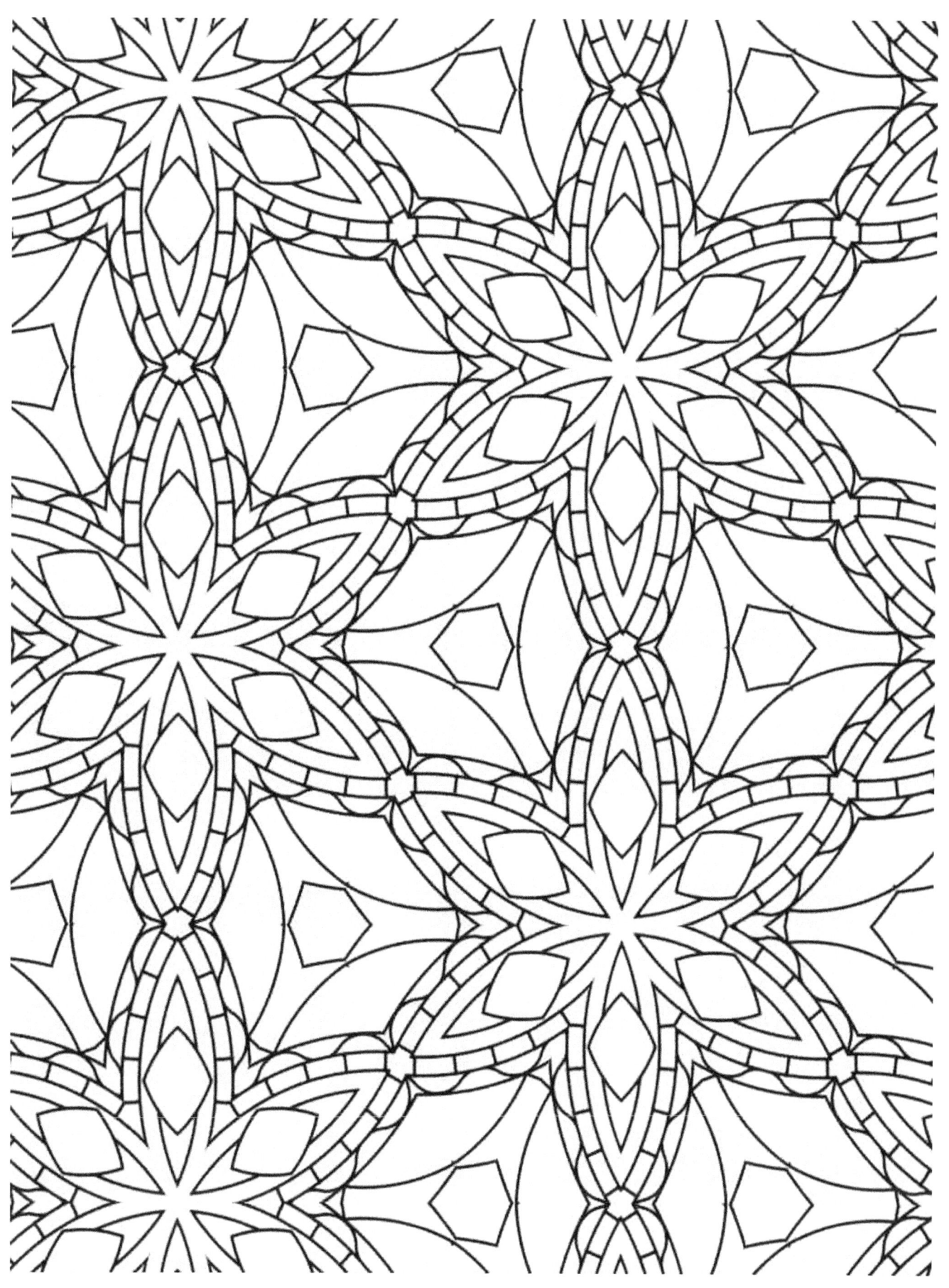

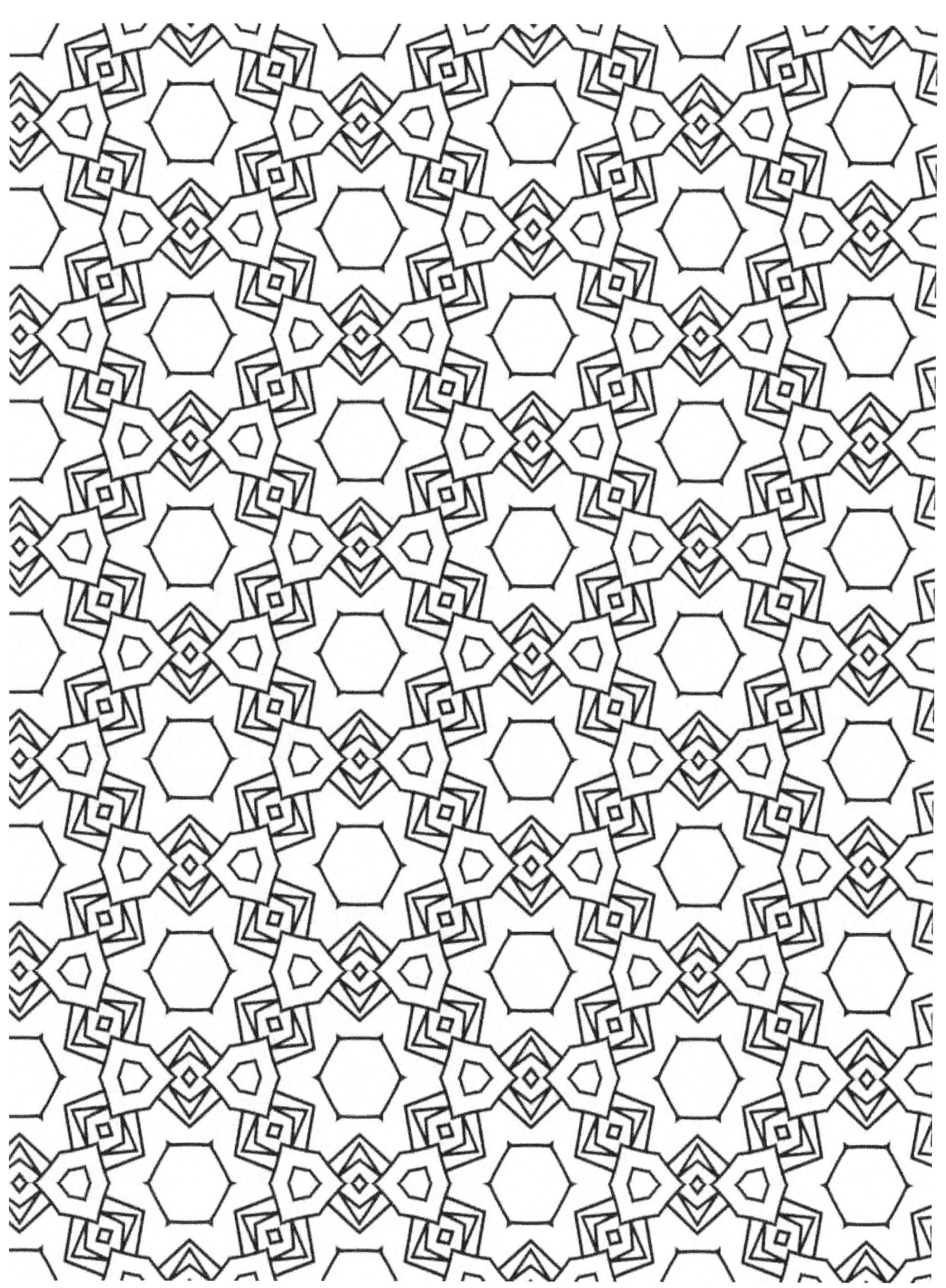

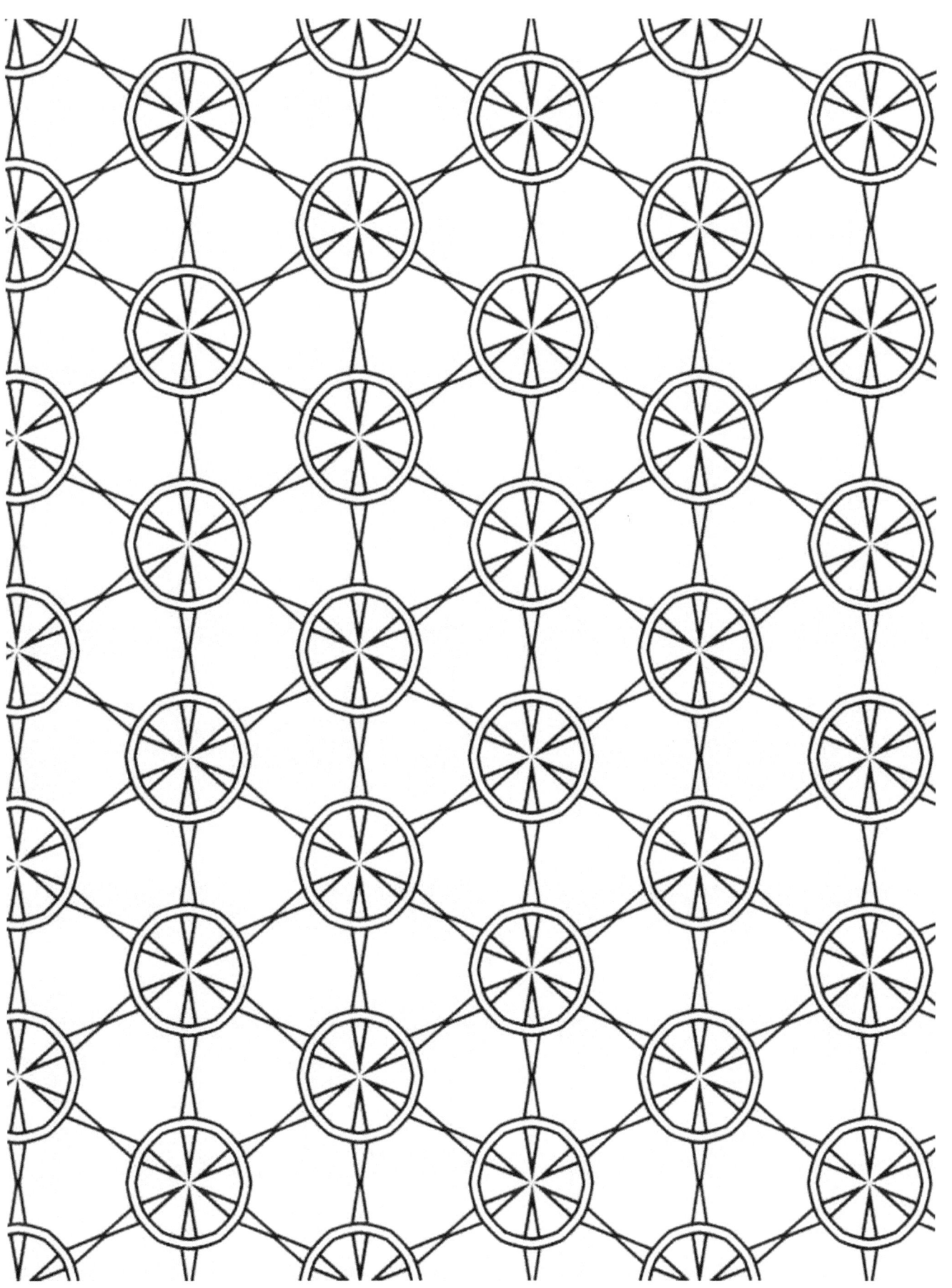

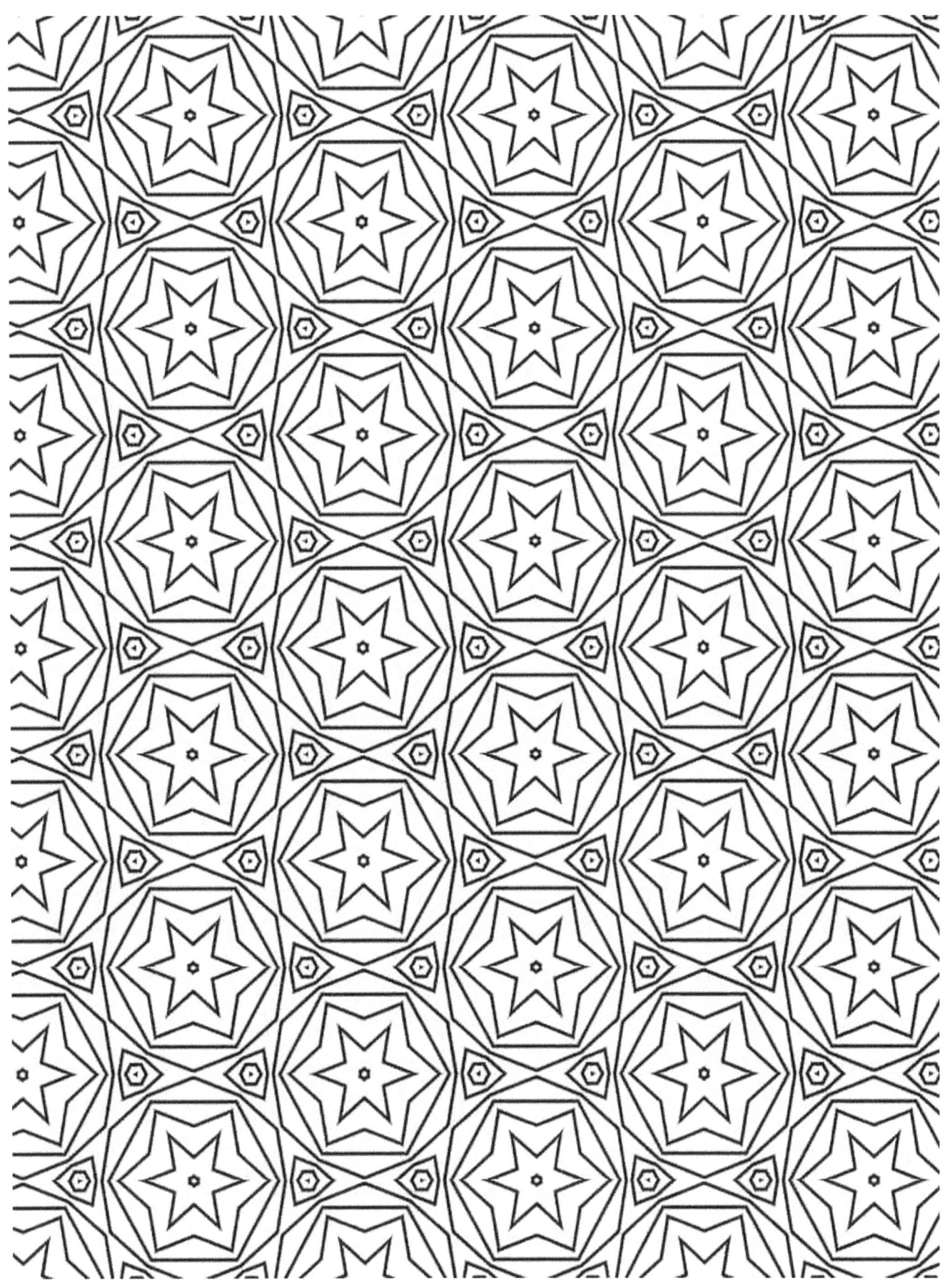

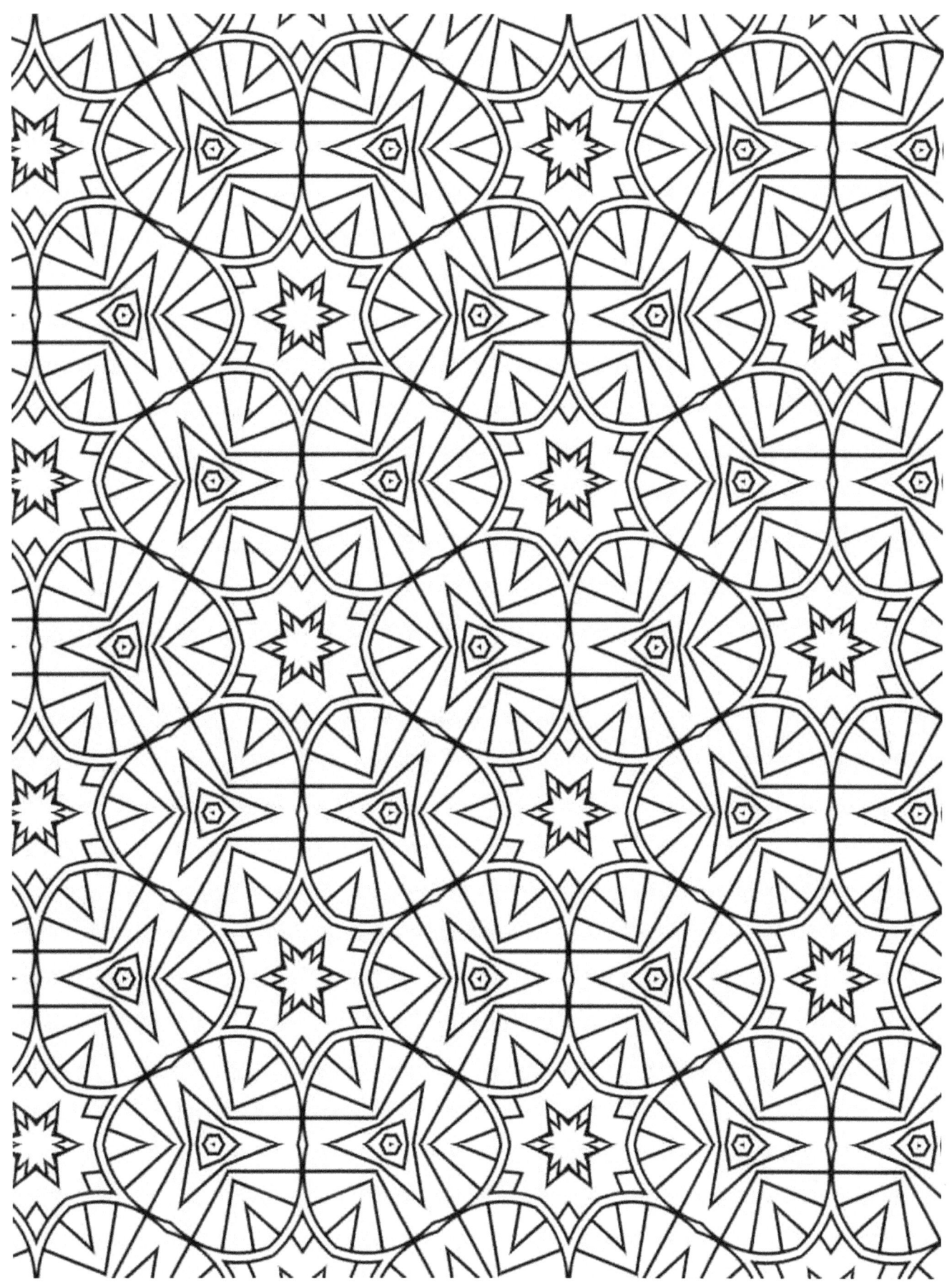

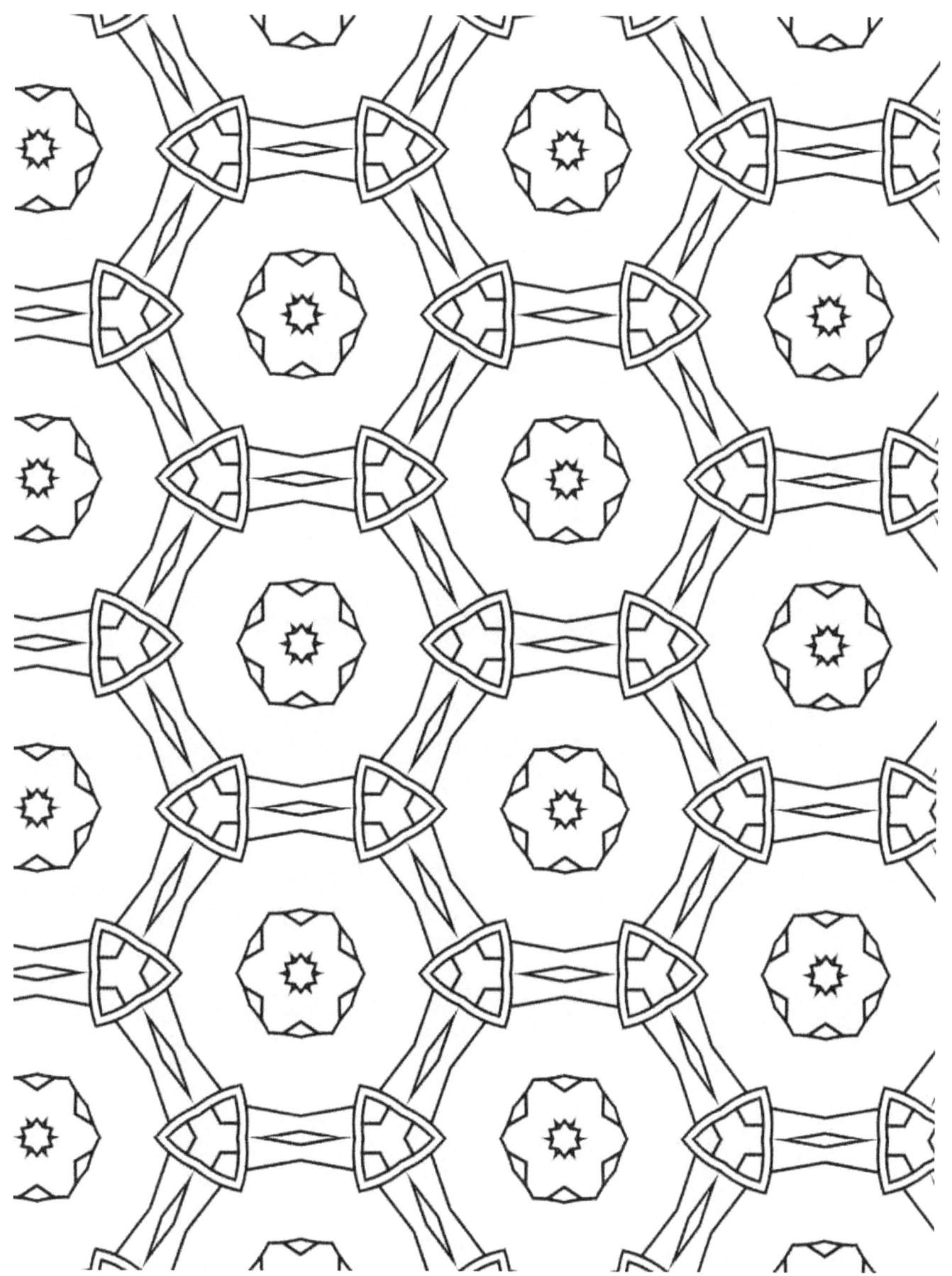

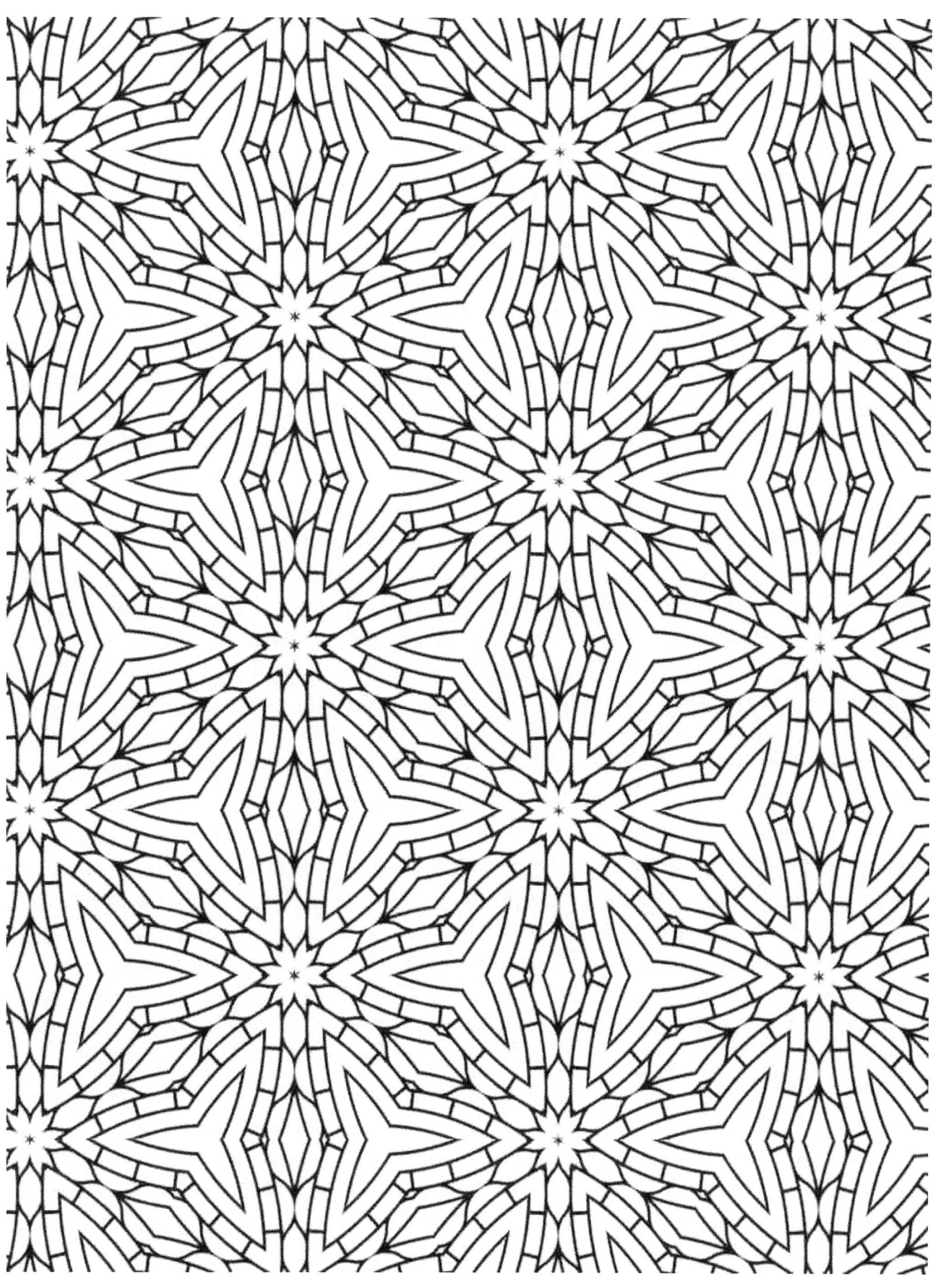

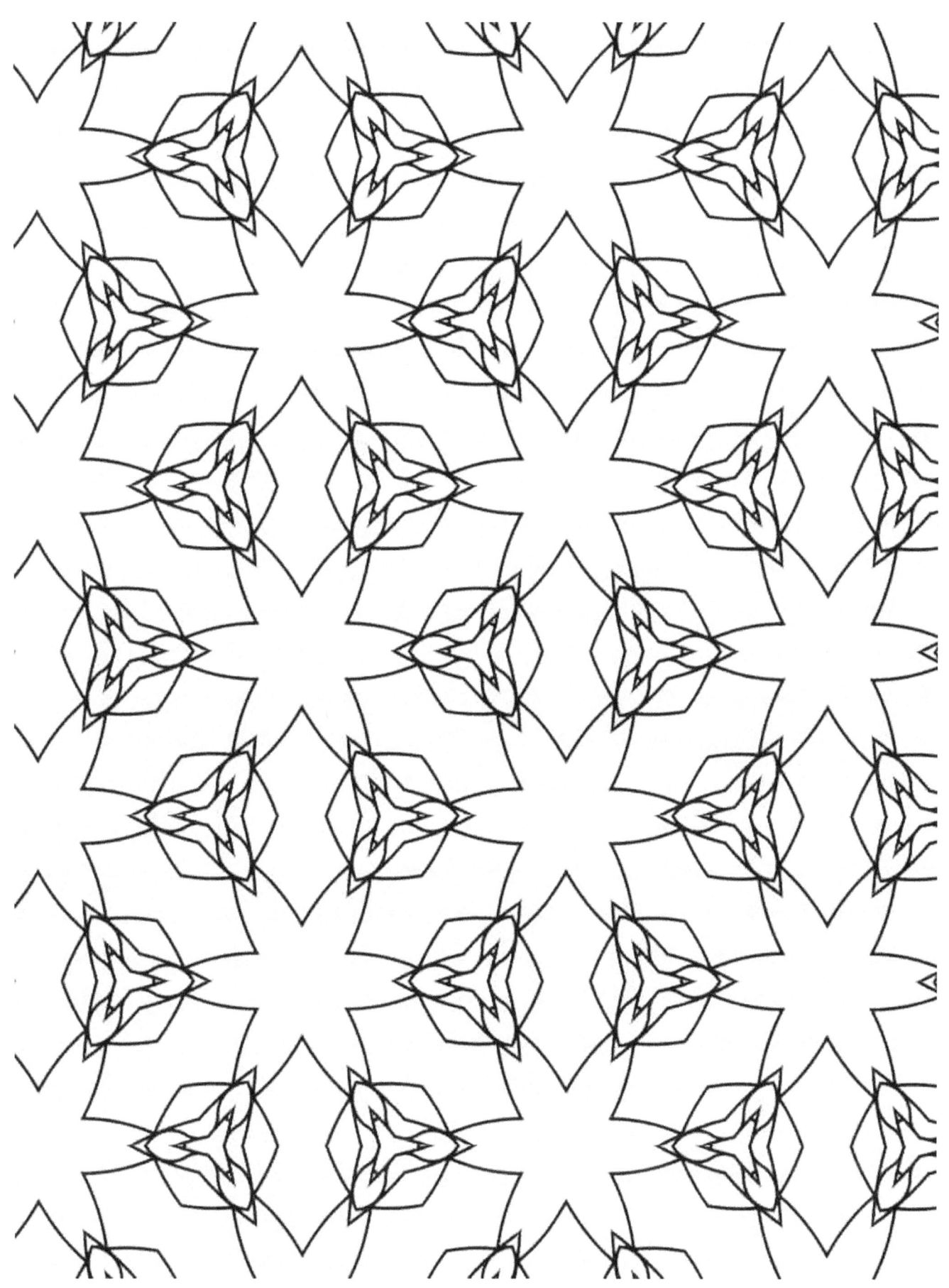

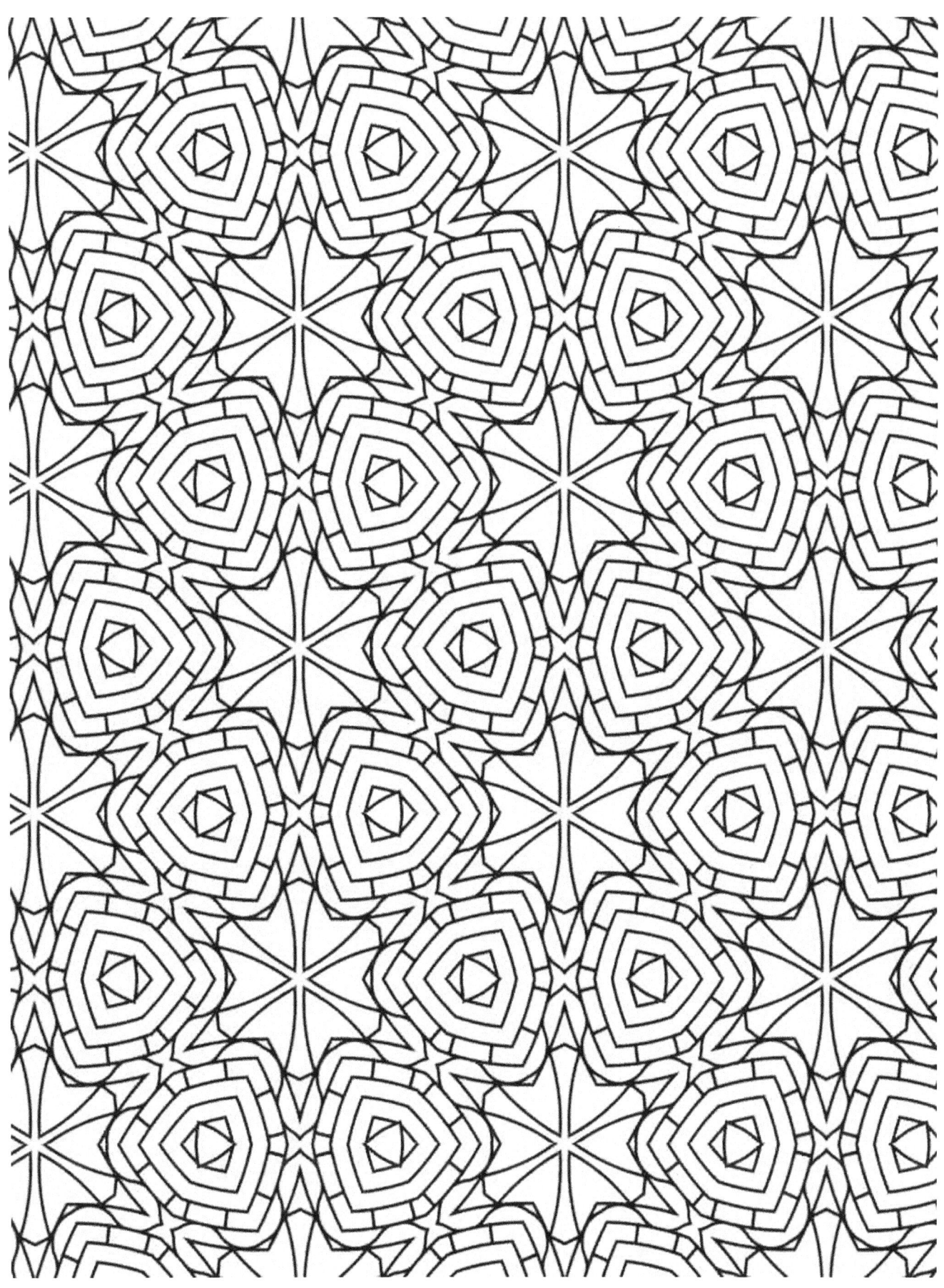

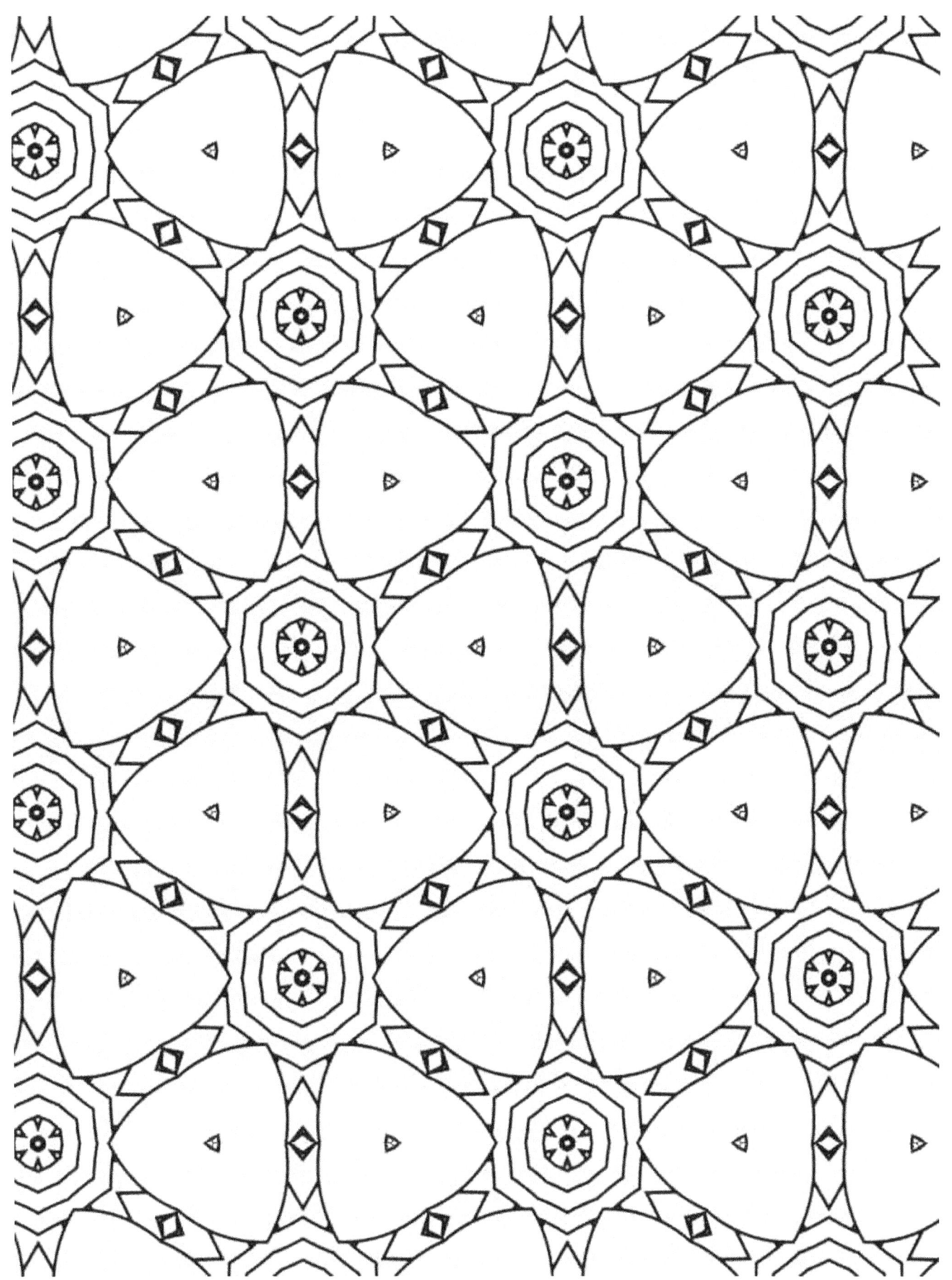

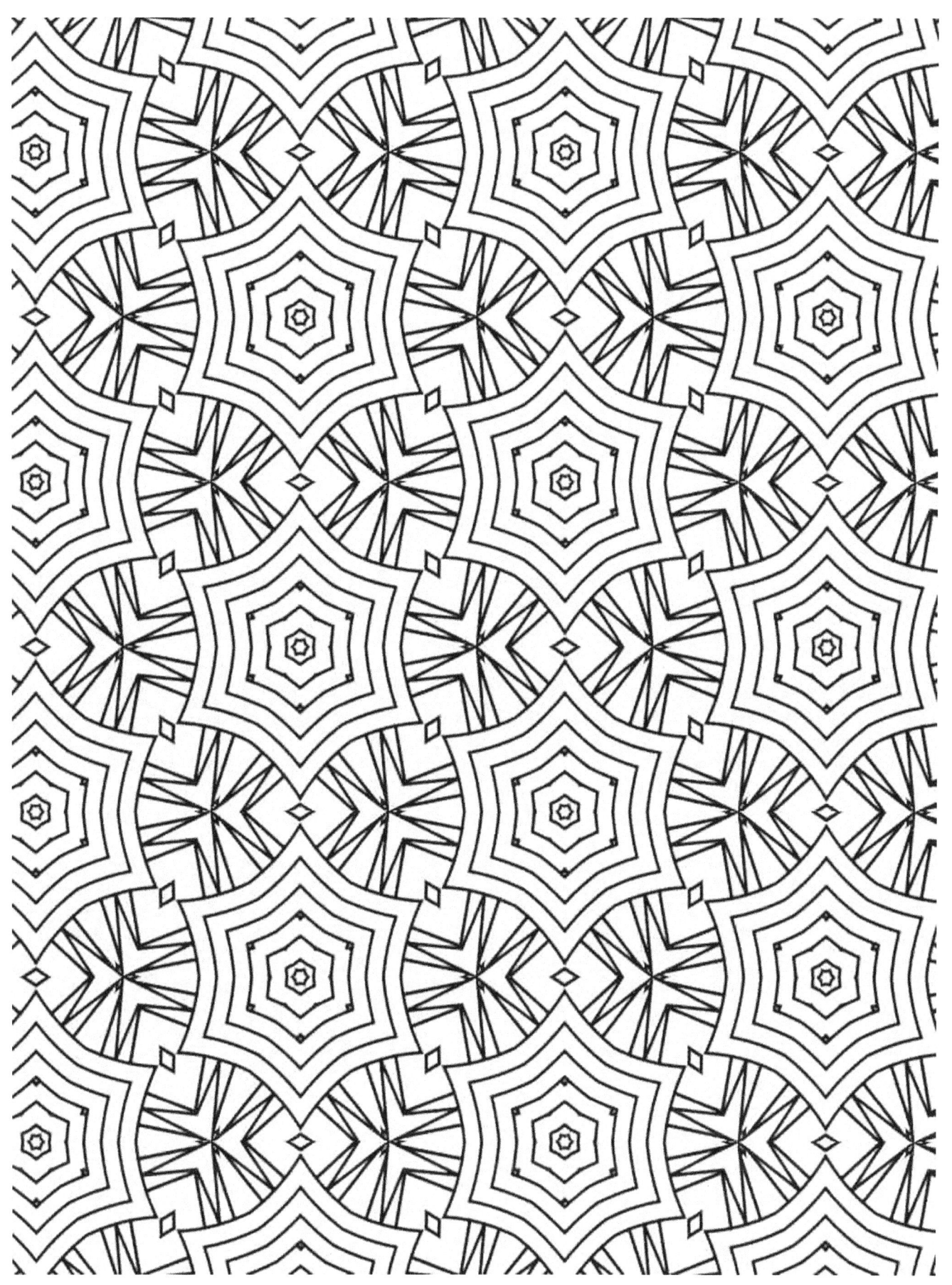

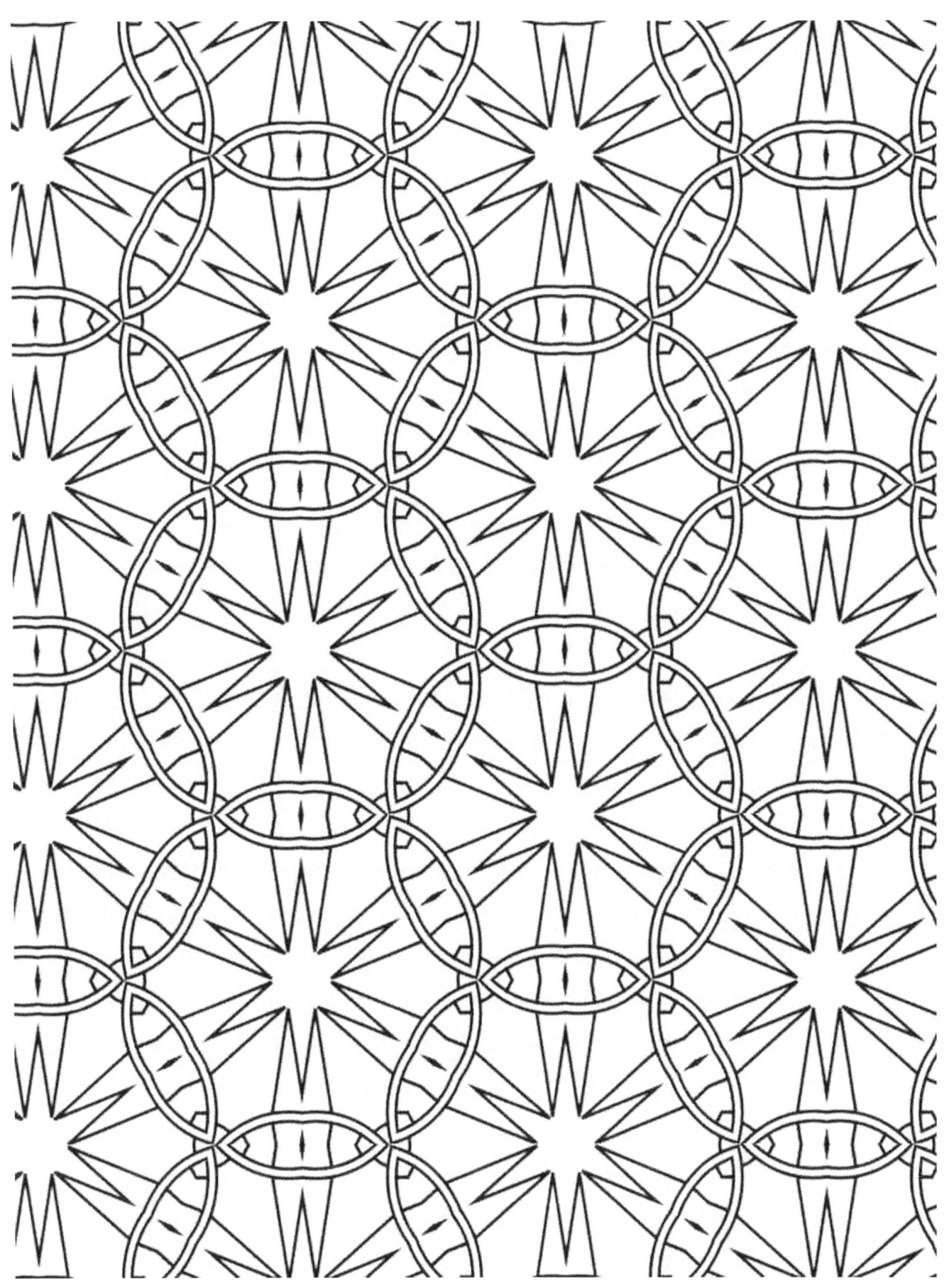

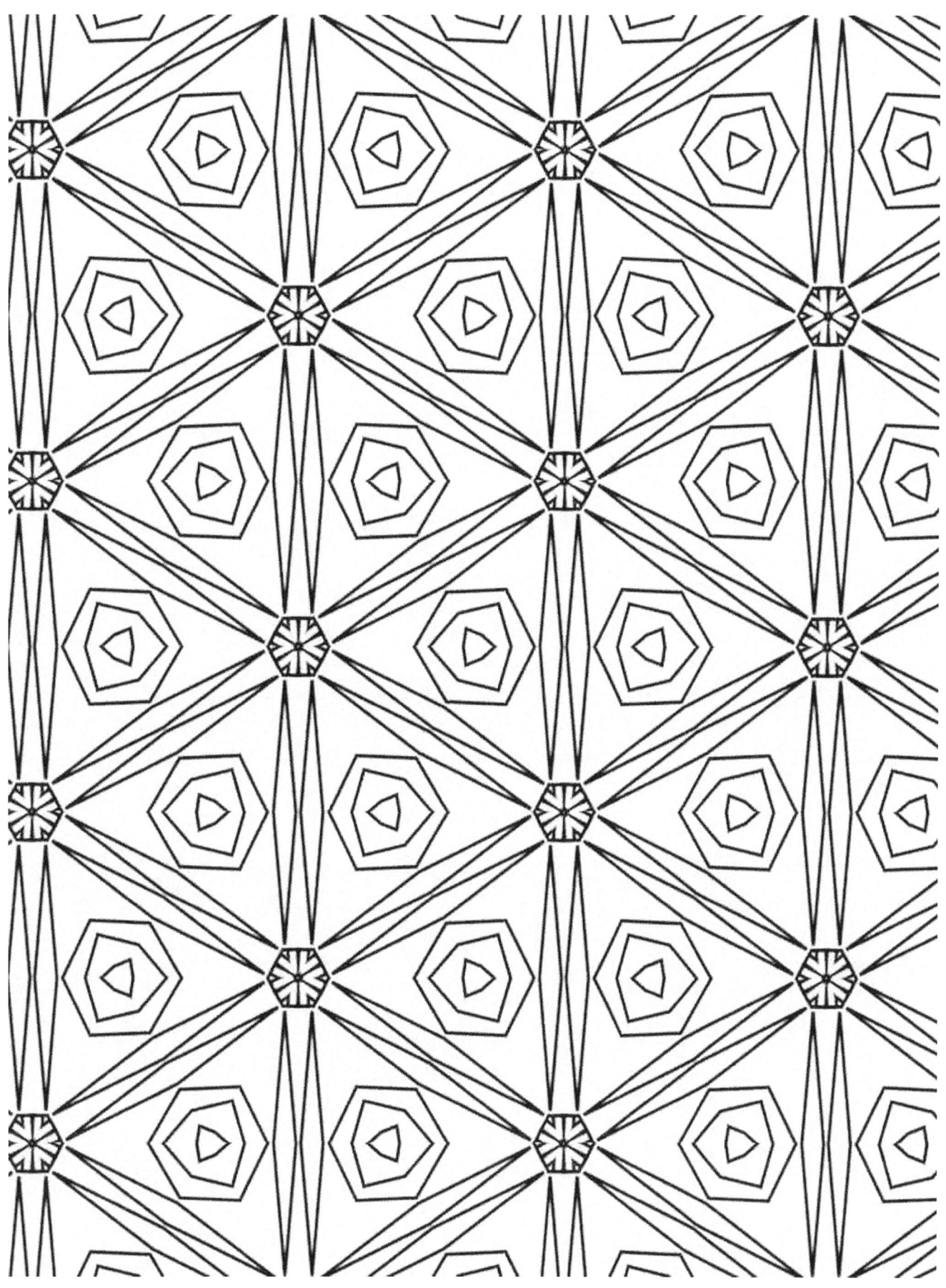

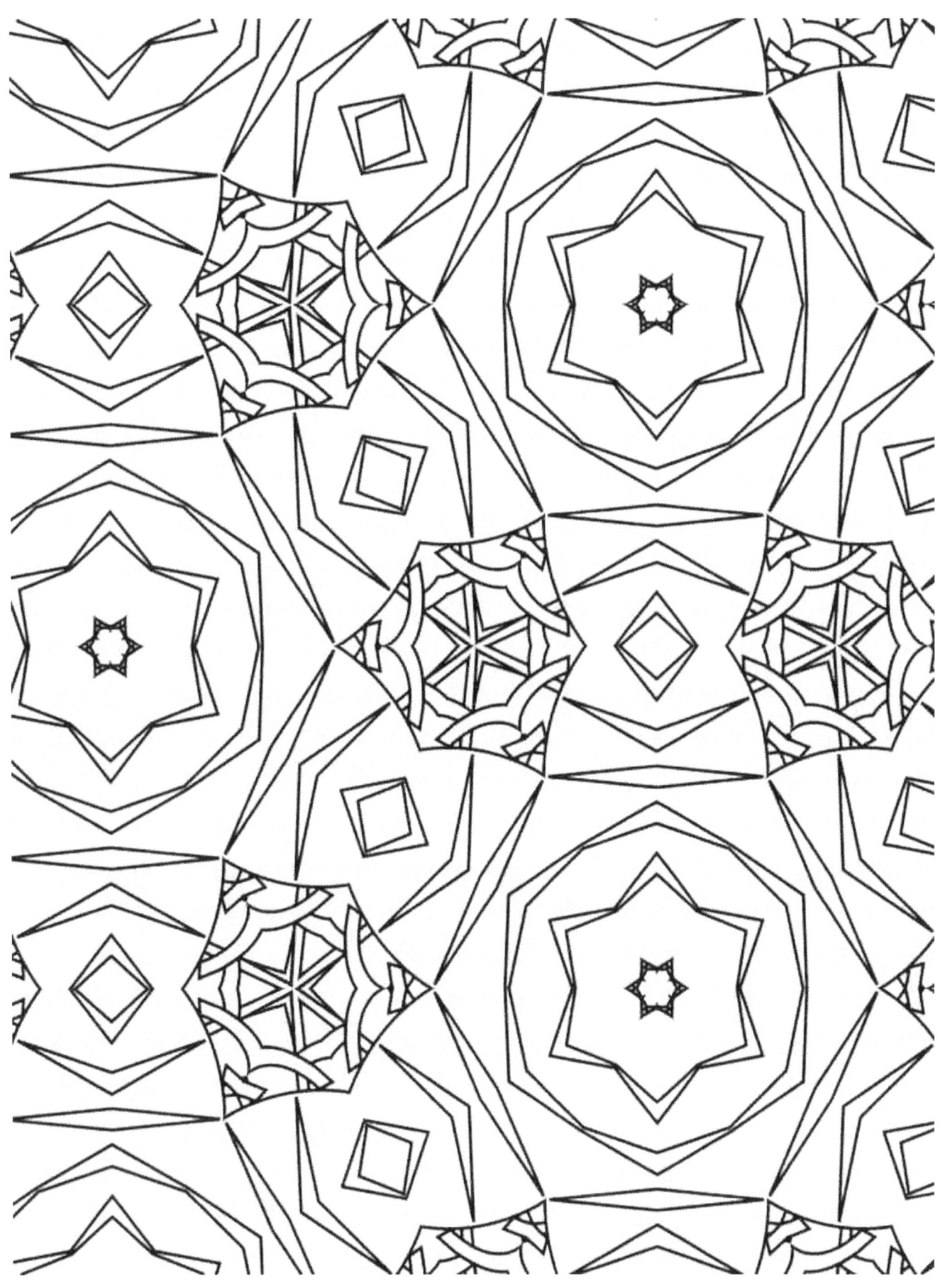

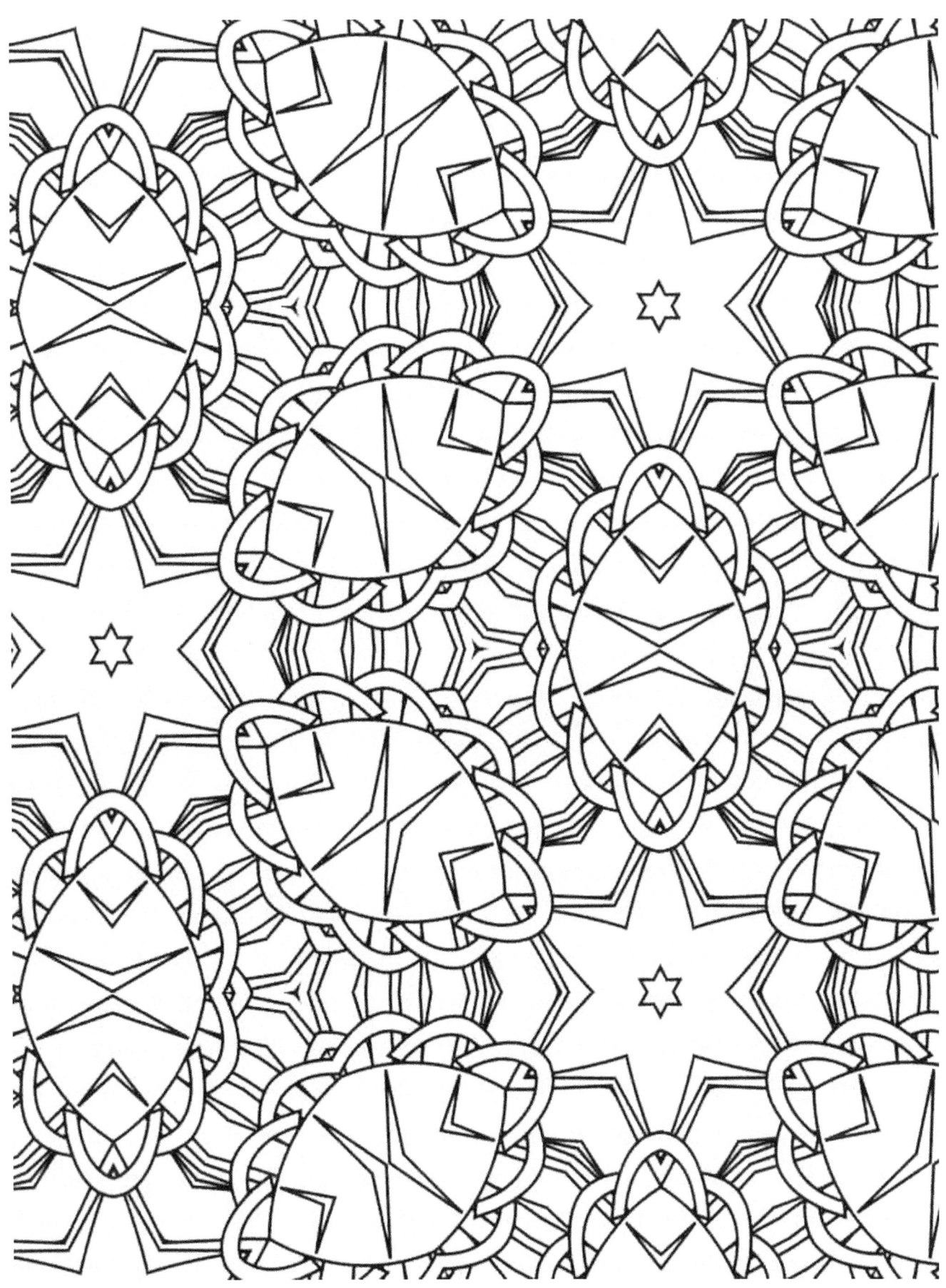

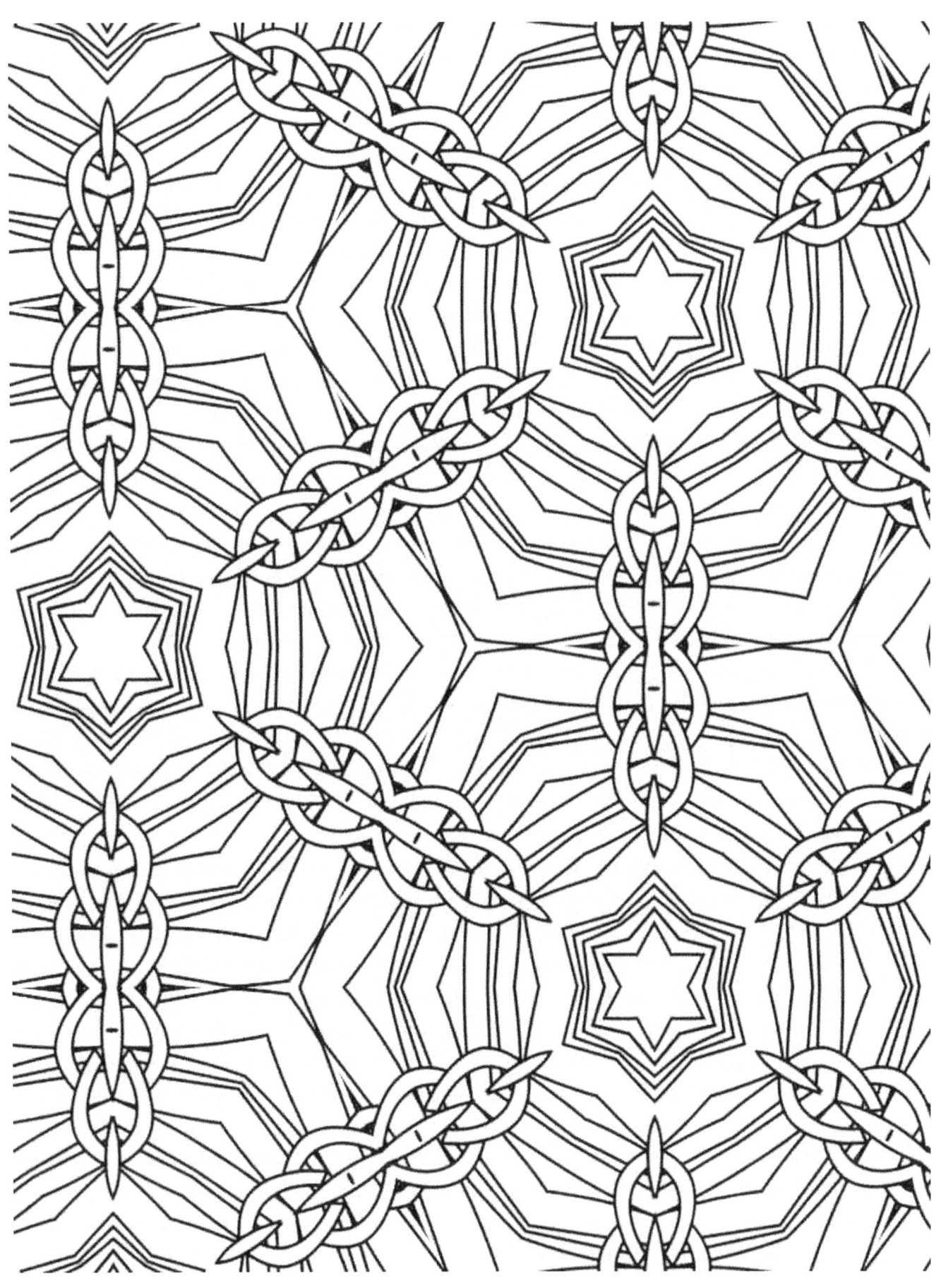

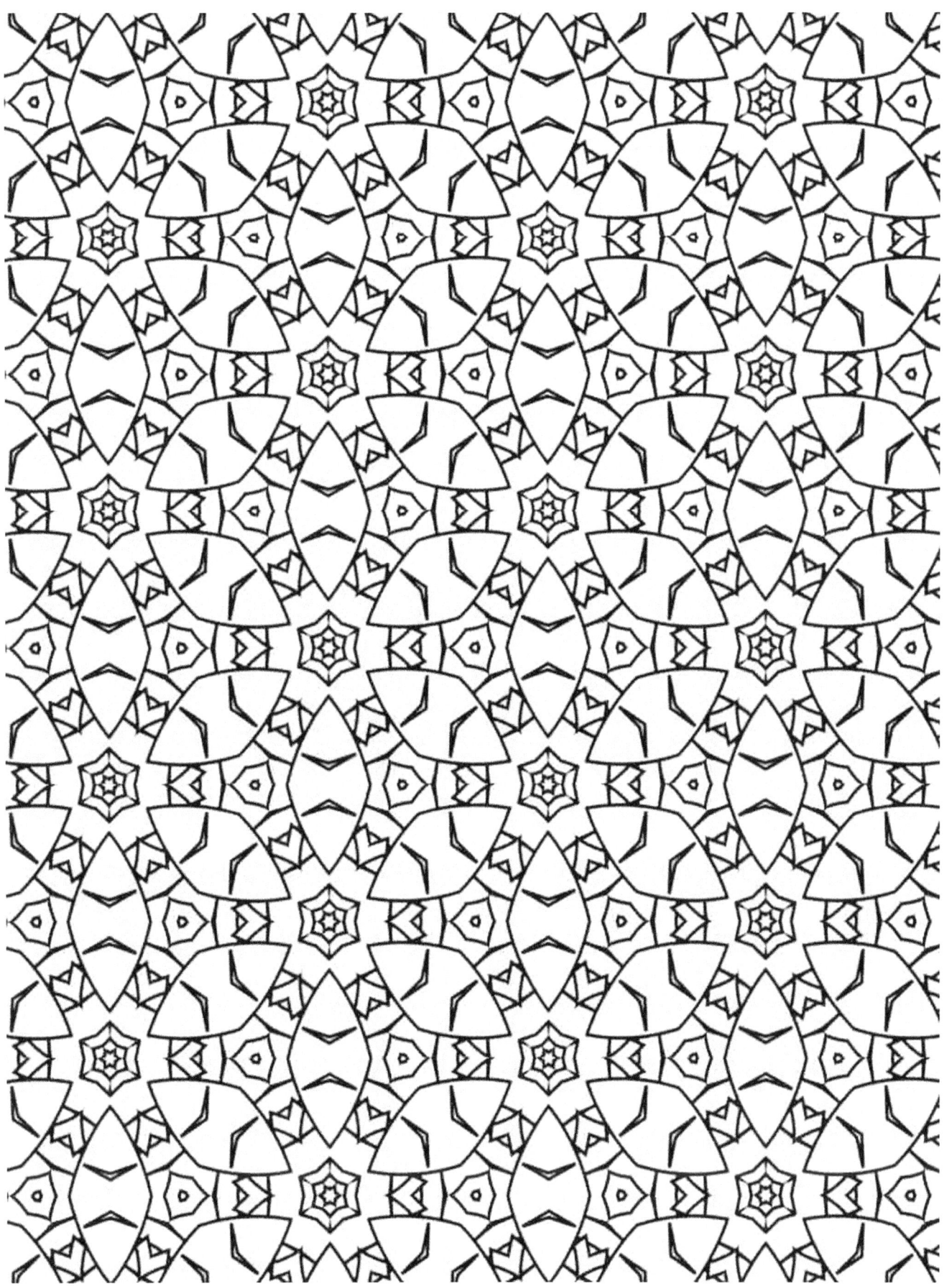

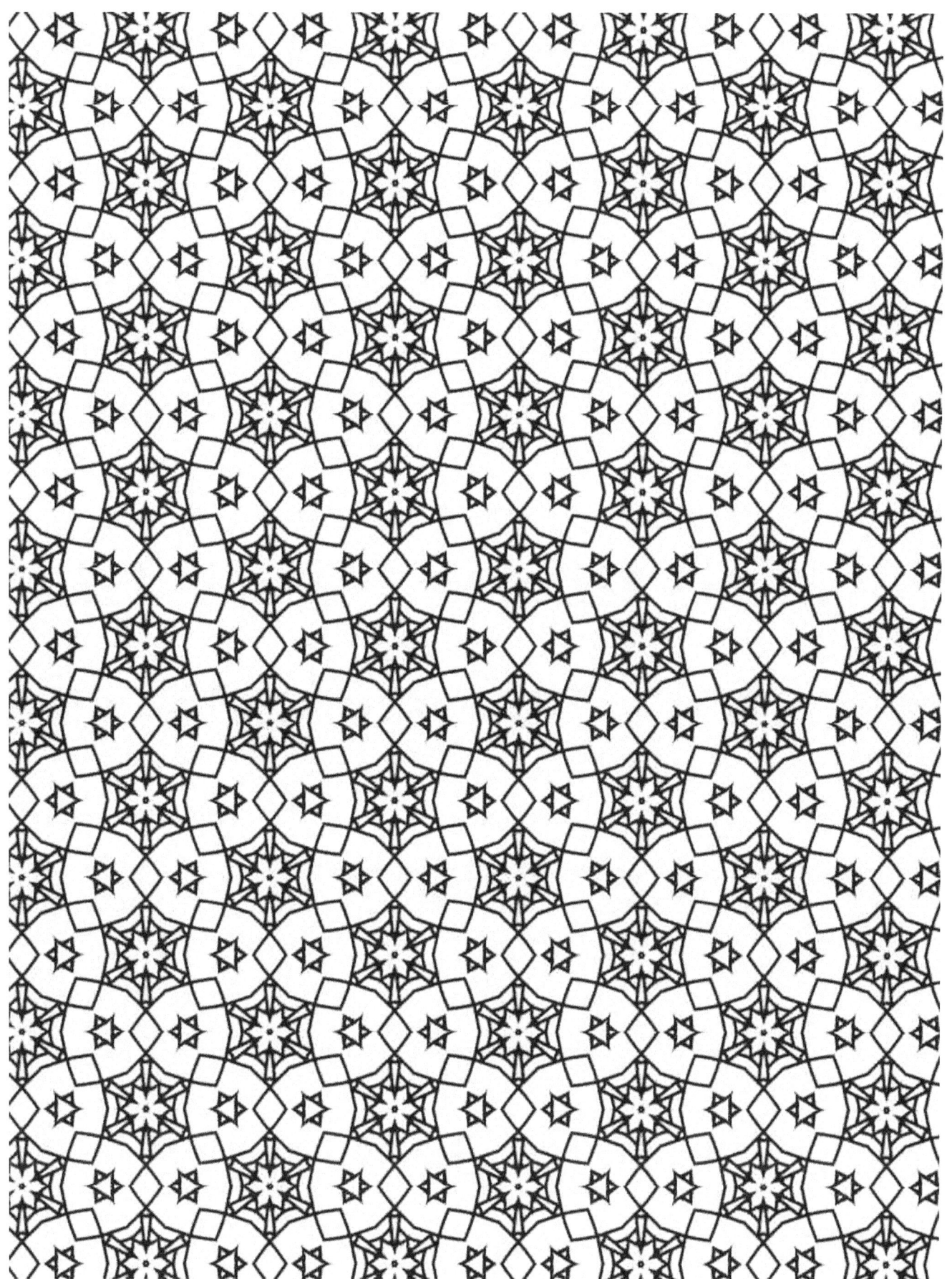

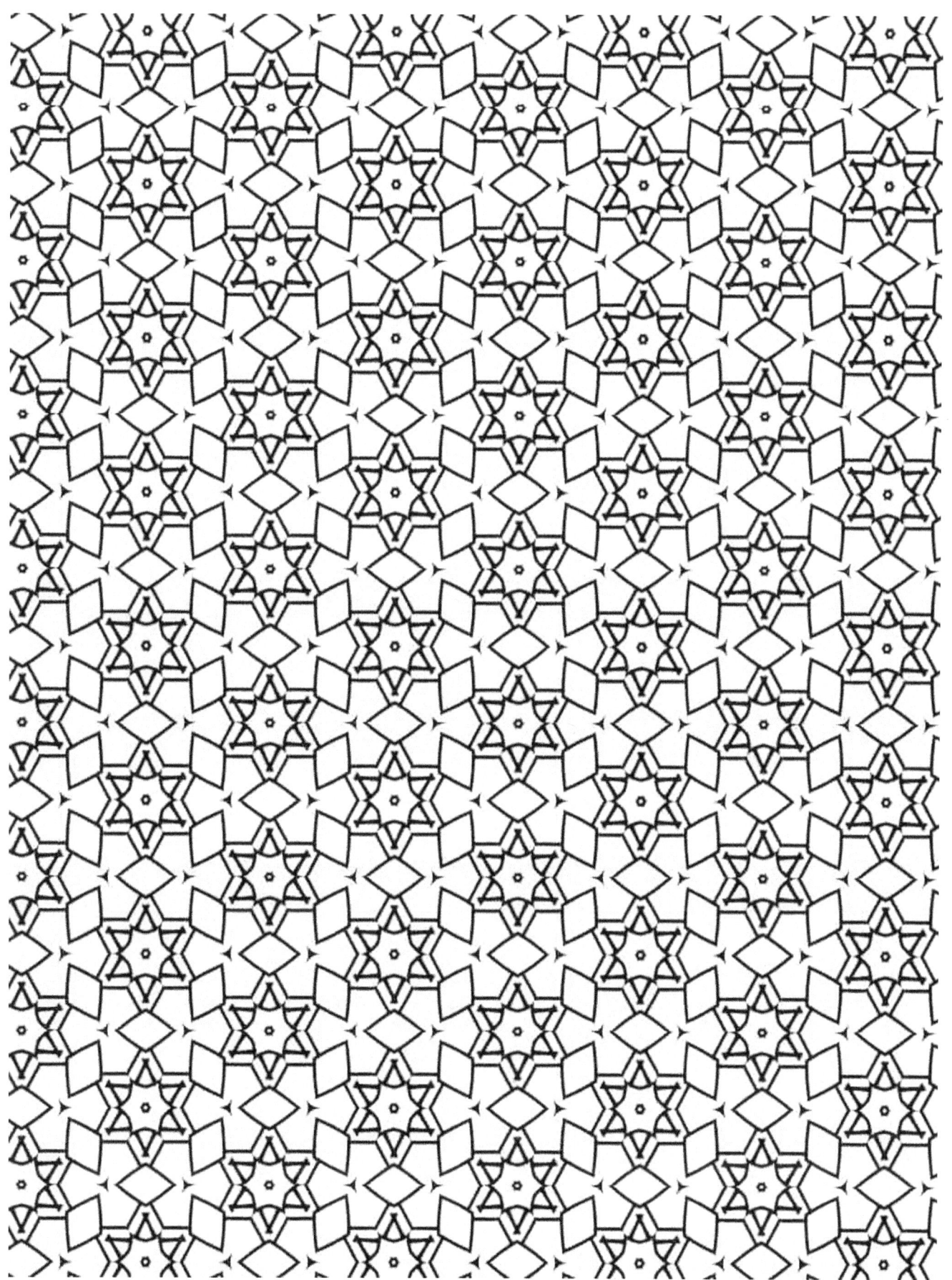

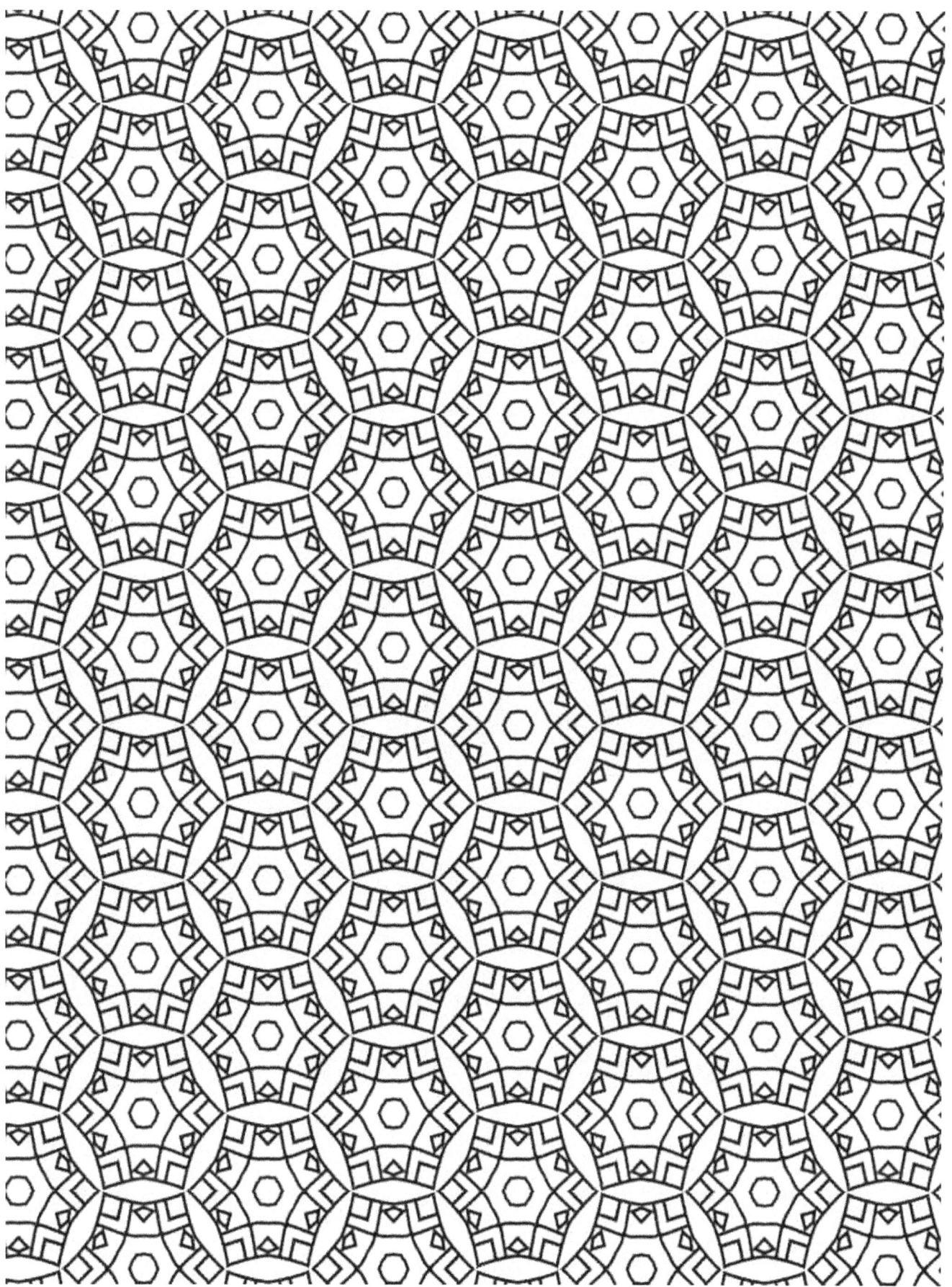

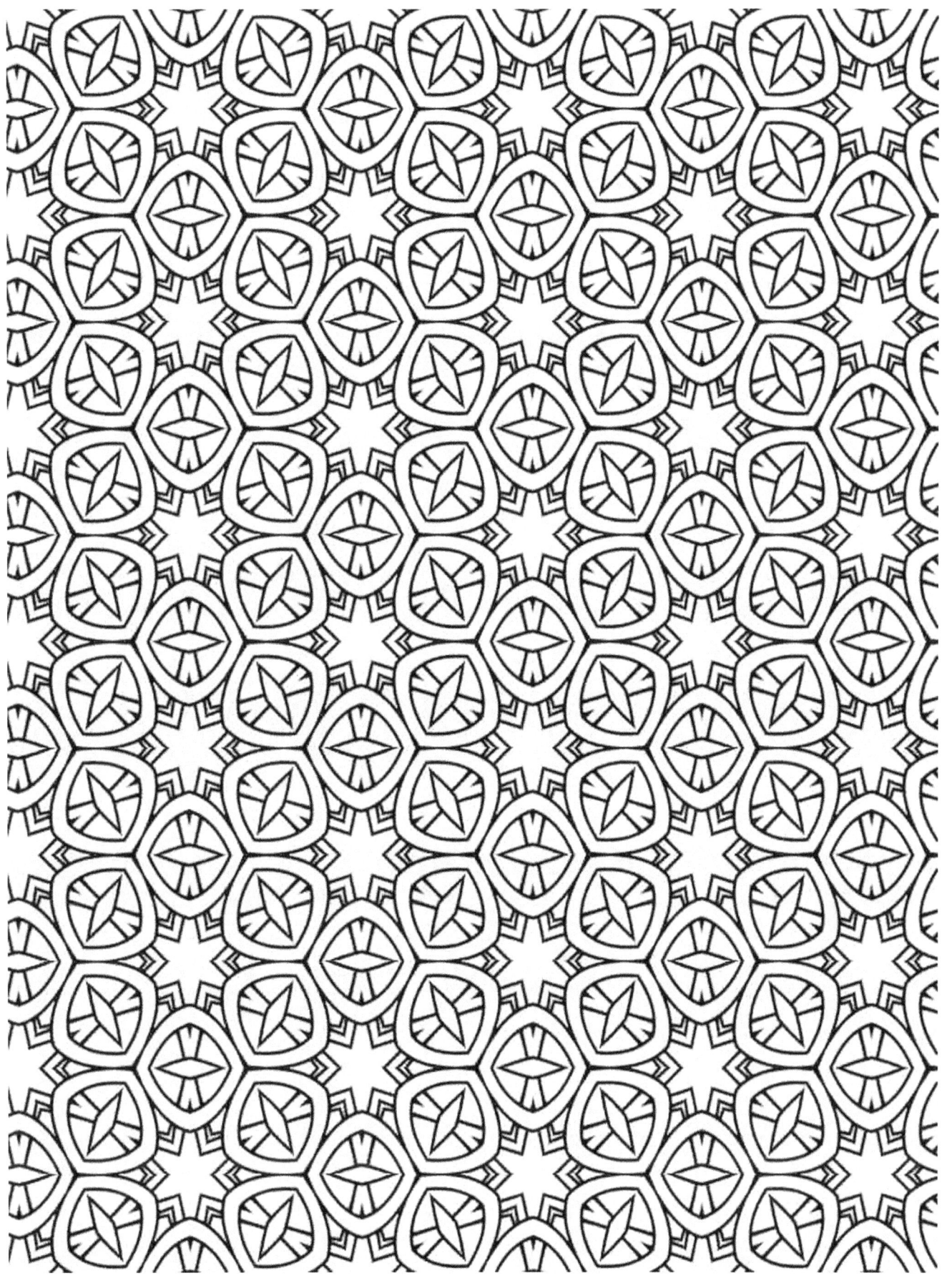

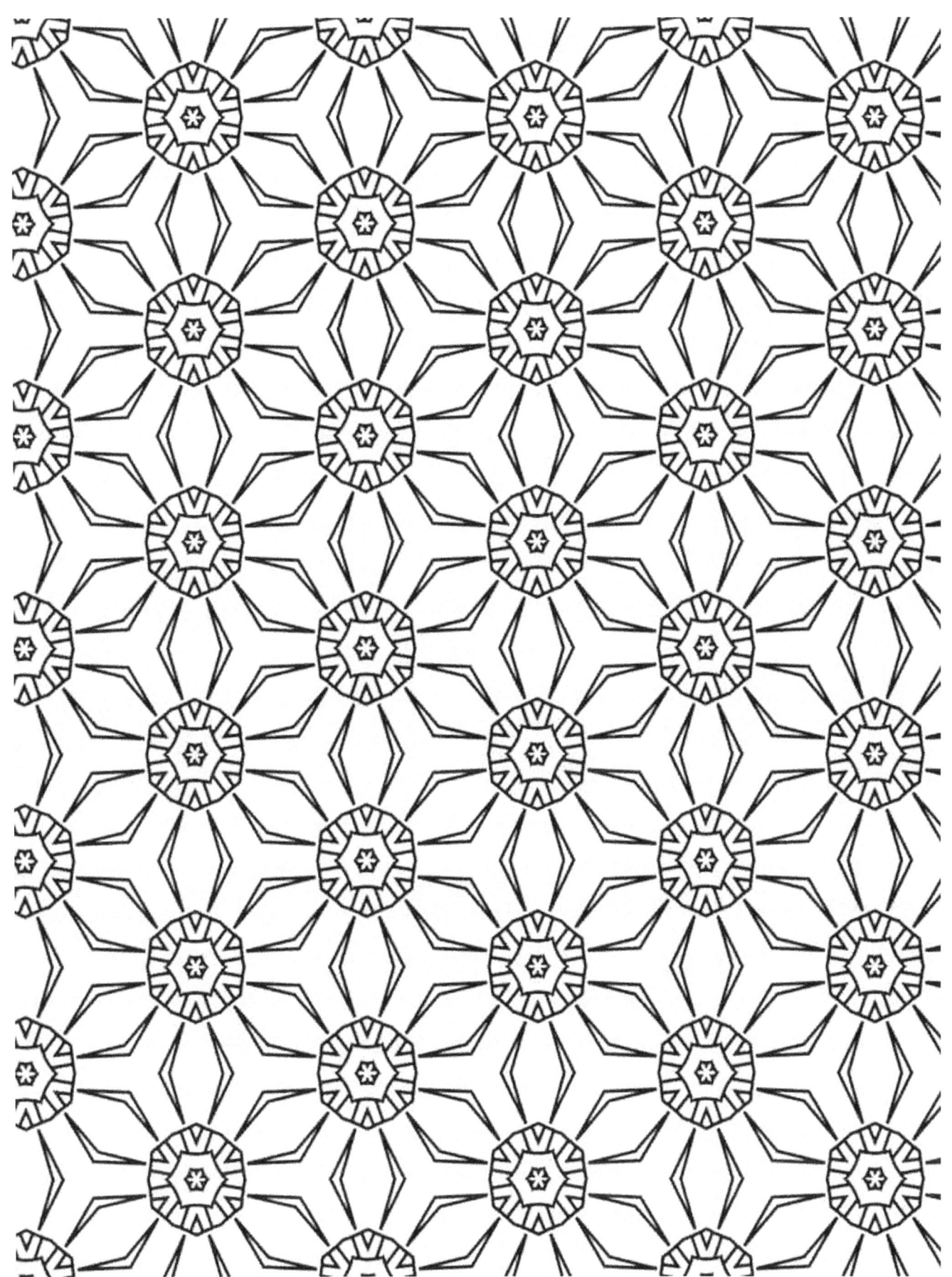

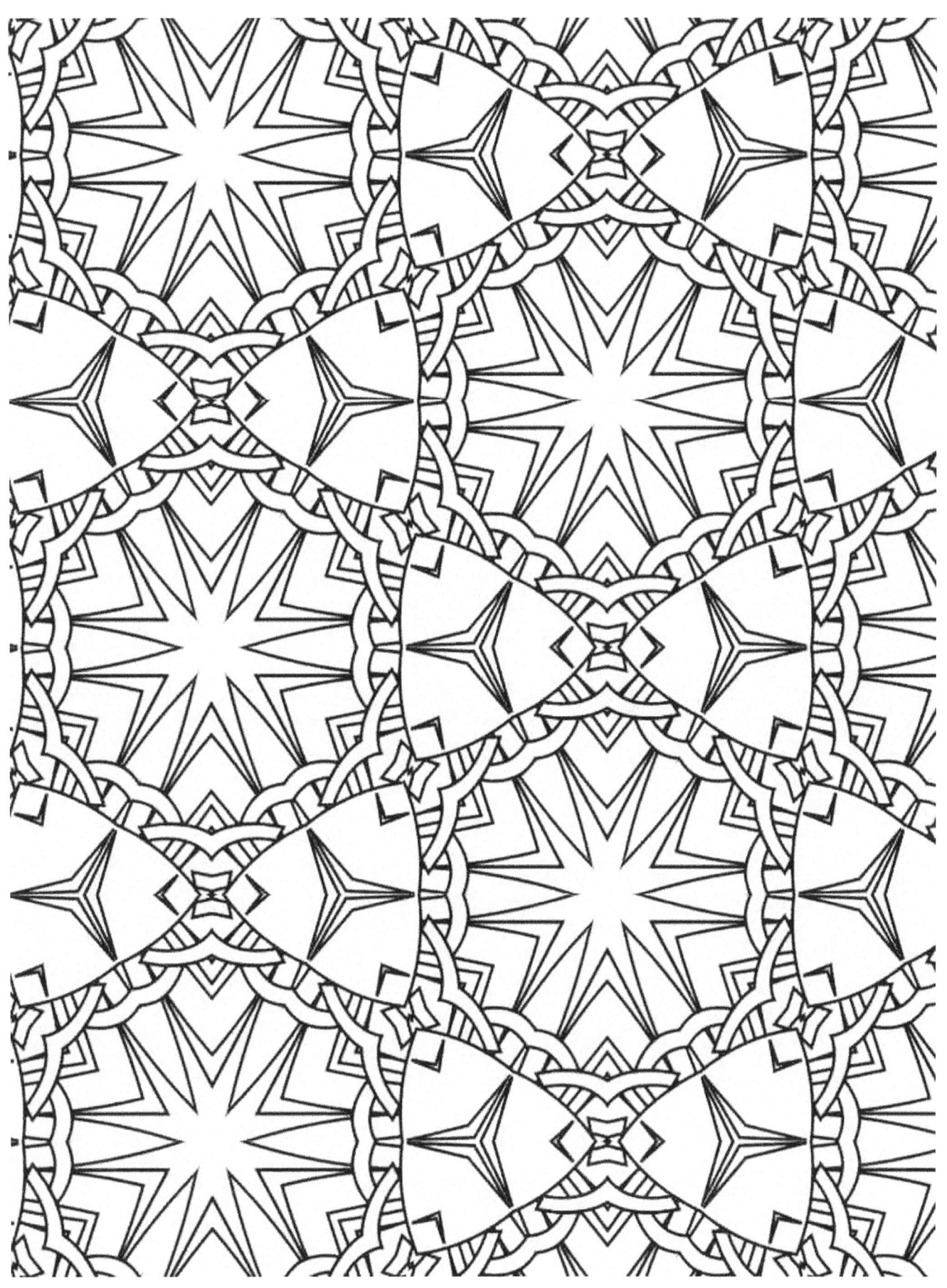

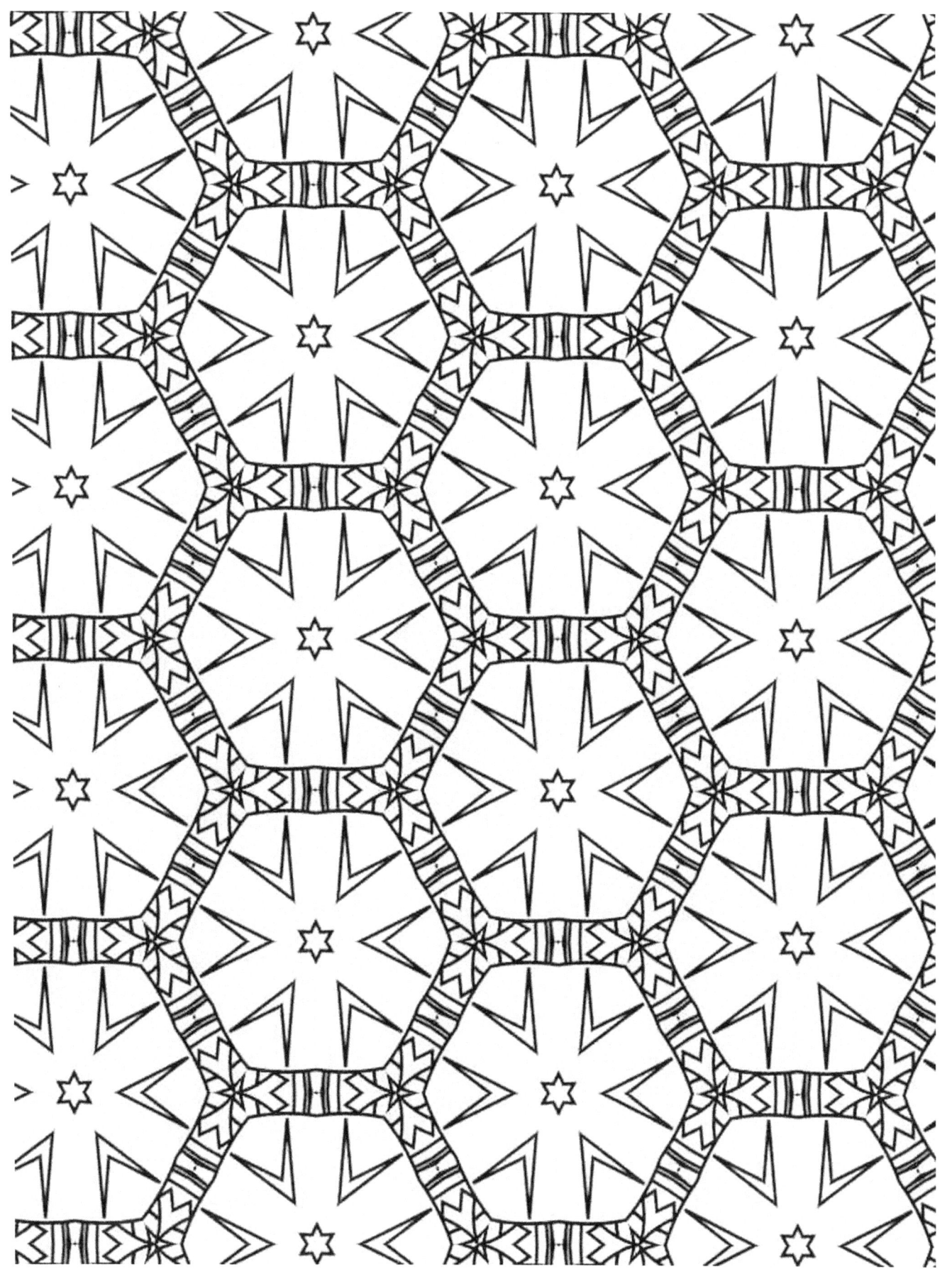

# THANKS

I hope you have enjoyed this book and it has brought you some peace through out your day.
I understand how crazy life can be sometimes so it's important to take 5 minutes everyday just for yourself, I hope this book has given you some comfort and a renewed sense of focus.

If you would like to receive a free download printable coloring book please use this link, just enter your name and an email address I can send your for book to. Thanks again.

## http://bit.ly/2cTSkyk

www.ingramcontent.com/pod-product-compliance
Lightning Source LLC
Chambersburg PA
CBHW080549190526
45169CB00007B/2702